FA

FANTASIA
Nisha Ramayya

GRANTA

Granta Trust, 12 Addison Avenue, London W11 4QR

First published in Great Britain by Granta Poetry, 2024

Copyright © Nisha Ramayya, 2024

A CIP catalogue record for this book is available from the British Library.

1 3 5 7 9 10 8 6 4 2

ISBN 978 1 91505 111 0
eISBN 978 1 80351 076 7

Typeset in Minion by Hamish Ironside

Printed and bound in Great Britain by T J Books, Padstow

www.granta.com

CONTENTS

~~~

now let's take a listening walk
gander to ground in the swallowing heart
in the figure-eight wake of a swan, how we sound

      our feet sea-skimming ears of the world, world the song
                                  this tune could be

          whorled surface
          suspend grammar

harp deep

out be

three for alice

Peace on Earth

She plays the whole world on the piano, as if her chromatic fleets
could meet the historical condition of fleets. There is no, there is
no, there is no conditionality of any kind, in the feel of her time.

The sound of playing together, really *playing* playing *together*
together, this band all clothed with ears. Fingertips foot-taps
puff-cheeks puckered with ears. Improvisation demands the nth
root of attention, when n is the number of *silent* silences they've
shared shared.

They play into the weight of histories, billowing sheets of sound,
twisting single-tracked history as their main cause, playing out
unsound pieces of possibly everlasting peace.

Sound is the possibility of sound and may not be sound itself.
Gross sounds arise and become subtle. Subtle sounds are
reabsorbed by the nascent state.

What's insistence on justice elsewhere in space? What's listening to
the sound of the spheres of the unborn, whilst the born are crying
here? Who? *Here!* Who? *Here!* Who? *Here!*

The audience claps in the room, elsewhere, *here on earth*. Sound is
wherever there is desire or vibration or clapping of any kind. Strike
that oh-om-OM!

An everlasting peace not caused by a shock, as like produces like,
as like destroys like, as if poison was the antidote for peace.

Oh-om-OM! The band's self-generating peace disregards the signature of time signature, overblows the treachery of the treaty. Oh-om-OM! An unsound peace for freedom elsewhere, *here*, for most freest elsewhere, *here on earth*.

A spatially-temporally disregarding atonality – ohhh – against the straight-lined centre-weighted militarized – ommm – for the dissonating other-regard of everlasting peace – OMMM!

Going Home

Aah, I, ah-aah

    I found

        I found I

            I found I, just didn't need

            I just didn't need, drone need, just didn't, ohhh

Sense organs cut through the tune this tune could be, just didn't need, this tune takes place inside. I what? Inside ear worm, in indignity.

Strings lay down staircase, impossible staircase, finding itself to be, going home, just didn't, getting. Anyone the sound of living alone. I found a way to be. I what? Be home. Drone unaccompanied. Anyone the sound of going home, supermundane and supreme.

You, the harp sunsets.

Blaze!

Harp sink us into ourselves, darkwash away the lie of heart's lowlights. Consciousness snail within us, silence, blaze! This tune upscales us monochromatically. Ah-aah, I-aye, um-what? Moon drive us on to electro-organic heights.

Impossible staircase, get us nowhere, get us raised up, ultralight beam lights.

To going home, to stolen home, to reclamation's getting nowhere, to down home, drill down, drop off whitebread heights. Brave background! Unscrew tune, invert ear drip, buttery be.

Electro-organic slide we sound. Sunset all the friends we knew. Sound play with luminosity, invite light to the party, sunrise too soon. Most freest silence!

Anyone else, the sound of self inverting self, cochlear lawlessness a means of getting away.

Anyone else laid down by lights, shells shot through with countersunk holes. Body boltholes, tube lit, home having home as its main cause.

Anyone else bodying home, body having home as its main cause. Snail shell battle cry, resonance following most subtlest sound.

Pour sand in ears to catch lightning strike. Trail sand through body home. Grit glissando, irritate ear, glass worm, too late.

My harp sings despite itself, squirms heartily, my sun sets, you-ooh, ow-aum, lightning struck my ears emit, I-aye, supreme-aye, ow-aum, emanate earwax homing device, I-um, this out be, this out be.

Out be.

Govinda Jai Jai

she! generates a party out of mantras!

somebody's face down at the party
too full too soon, i.e., ready to evolve

syllabic bloat, causal stress when
I! bursts in

the aloneful party falls *apart* in a field
together, *apart*, together

in a field of one, a battlefield, the supreme I ayes

she! generates a chorus of skull cracks

subtle sound descends into chorus, *one must be identified*
with the sound of the spheres, oh-ow-aum!

sound out cracks in the foundations
of the field buttercups in cracks
not a gladness too soon

gladness! only exists only too soon

anyone else clapping, everybody comes in
on the clap only too soon, gladness comes
in between claps there are fields and fields
of buttercups in between claps battlefields

we! is herded in claps

existence is the gross effect caused by vibrations
of the existential potential

> *one is identified with the whole world*
> *and thus indifferent to it*
> *one must identify the void in the whole world's heart*
> *with the void in one's own heart*

the party changes its tune

I the sound of living together
> *I-aye, ow-aum*

tickle the spark in disharmonic intervals
> *you-ooh-oh*
> > *cup, chin, aah!*

in a field somebody's falling
buttercup tickles my living alone
falling in buttercups alonefully when

she! little mothers of the phonemes

all clothed with ears germinating worlds
to keep word-bound speech-clad lovers apart
> phonetic mitosis on the tip of the tongue

in a field somebody's tidying the cowherd
gladly tidies chart success of any kind, everybody isn't
victorious over life, i.e., resigning it willfully

the claps slow down for emphasis, failing rights
of primogeniture face down in the interval

before the last vibration
the last clap back

our dissolution is the pinpricking of tensions
to a divine ear tension's homogeneity

The Divine Ear must be dissolved!

flower cup, seed vessel, wreath of words

Misting the ivy, her groin chakra is at 47 per cent. The green hearts of the leaves turn as pale as their almost white outlines. She considers phoning her mother for advice, but the thought of speaking, of hearing herself speak, of compelling body to expend more breath than simply breath; of pressing lungs, laryngeal muscles, organs of articulation and pronunciation; the thought of those latent sites of her own voice inside her, of interiority exiting the body without smell, stain, or structural rigidity; of her interiority encountering her mother's across space-time like one's own serpent rising out of one's own body to meet another's serpent rising out of another's body, to lick, to twist, to bolt. The green hearts of the leaves turn brown as their seat of desire.

the beyond of teaching teacher voice

TEACHER: You may begin.

SOME MISSIONARY: Why not then worship my *boot*?

TANTRIC METAPHYSICIST: Boot is body. Body is boat. Why not then sail through bliss; why not then tune your body to the interruptions swimming below, the disruptions gusting above? You pave paradise and walk ungrounded.

SOME MISSIONARY: Why not then *worship* my boot?

TANTRIC METAPHYSICIST: Sound is deathless; the gramophone of the universe is never at rest. Science must invoke the analemmic swan!

SOME MISSIONARY: Why *not* then worship my boot?

TANTRIC METAPHYSICIST: . . .

TEACHER [off stage, from above]: Nine hours and ten light years later, the Tantric Metaphysicist is still alive and swimming strongly. Star-jellies, attracted by the hum of a held tongue in the static unmanifest, gather round. The exam was over.

∧∧∧

try as close as you can to consciousness without memory

 the perpetual mantra, body seeder

  oṁ hrīṁ strīṁ huṁ phaṭ ‖

 disarticulate wildfire shuttering up and down
 your sevenfold spine: *now! now! now! now! now! now!*
 now! &c.

jammy ricochet, can't last

following ten million dinner parties

Z asks, at a dinner party, what is our shared ancestral knowledge?

This question discharges a circuit I've leapt from whilst skidding, drawn in sand and leaky pens, discovered in family trees and histories of migration; a spiral I've attempted to erase from my body and poetry, asserted in writing, tried to break to seek liberation; a map I've tracked to find community and networks of various kinds (social, poetic, political) and that's led to this dinner party in London for South Asian women and nonbinary people. The gathering itself is a palimpsest of circuits, spirals, maps. Some of our lines intersect and coordinates stack; we recognize similarities within the monotonizing difference that's imposed on us. Some lines diverge and coordinates repel, hazarding the contingent collectivity of the question, so it's gorgeously, alarmingly charged, even now. I can't share what anyone else said; I can't respond without swerving.

> A string of pearls between fantasists; papa's mama posing as a moustachioed warrior in a jodhpur and top-hat combo, an Olympic diver taking off from a footstool, the polka-dot cravat in his unspent matrimonial ads found in a storeroom in Hyderabad, and the ghosts of four teenage girls in turbans and lace gowns spotted in the woods of Strachur.

> How would it feel to have a relationship to the past that is not mediated by old photographs? For example, the tattoos on the arms of the women administering bucket baths.

> Or does the mediation itself confer meaningfulness; like, there's nothing here that didn't come through you, there's nothing there that I would claim?

Do white poets have ancestors?

Who belongs?

ask not what nor who you
fancying likeness droop
to red thread and inkhorn
breed some flew humbly
I'm performed unilaterally

measure out life in parties
material immaterial and
spiritual possessions scrap
for laughs or shave for
levelling stinking giveaway

*Z asks, how do we articulate South Asian erotics, where do
we begin?*

a hunk of tamarind pulp
plonked by a structure
held up by Cinderella blue
columns a cloudy child
hiding amongst buttercups

involuntarily my voice it
plays back the shit
eating sandalwood paste
eating Tantric guru
straightforwardly at sea

your one-word answer as a
cabinet of curiosities you
offer what I cannot find not
knowing what's mine roots
broke every pot on the terrace

She ate like a bird before she died. She sooks bones for marrow. She ate like a pig after she had children. She tells time by whistles and space by the scalds on her arms. She sandbags her body against the flood of words. Her mouth is the apocalypse. She was beset by the family name. She made pickles in a locked room. She pokes bellies and pinches inches. She took a little hookah at parties. She learns through tasting. She loved curd and sugar. Her citizenship obscured her class position. She couldn't remember how she used to make it. She goes missing after her daughter is born. She deserves it. Her green tongue is a bridge between the way and waves. She treats her body like an air plant. She hosted a dinner party after bringing her first child home from the hospital. Her singleness was a false face, what she hid would eclipse her. She looked very chic eating ice cream. She could make riverfish cutlets and three kinds of dal. She raised her children to be weight conscious. She wouldn't reveal all the ingredients in the recipe. She teleports ball gags. Her mother died of cancer, from poisoning incurred at work, perhaps. She spilled crème caramel on her lehenga. She incinerated her taste buds and needs even more mirch. Her blue tongue is synecdochic for self-sacrificing love. She drank herself to death. She wouldn't let the little boy sit down on her chairs, her maidservant's son. She sold her wedding jewellery in secret. She was raised by motherless mothers. She remembered Belgian chocolates. Her throat chakra will not tolerate abnegation. She developed a pimply rash from eating too many mangoes. She bypassed her husband and served all kinds of meat. She treats her body like a dustbin. She dreams of being the obstruction inside her own bowels.

if nothing is salvageable
but phenotypical vow
asymptotic brown erotics
rankling in old-new ills
I notice I'm caterwauling

to write lines that might
touch without being
touched without tickling
the scales of justice
inwardness and opening

to take without extracting
in slow motion tunnel
through floral foam react
to bumtrails by dimpling
drift apart decussating in ash

caterwauling

An image of women's and children's bodies, all higgledy-piggledy.
An abstract painting in, say, a sunset wash, orange swept in watery
layers and allowed to run down the canvas, pooling and drying to
form a line at the bottom. You can imagine the artist dipping claw
sheaths in red and blue-green ink and flinging them at the canvas –
so many little nicks. A smattering of dashes and purls in double-split
complementary colours. Do you see writing, I think I can see writing
but I can't make out words. You seem unsettled, what did you read?

Inclusion as a snake pit for the ones who don't want to belong, won't
macerate in the venom of duty, stamped and separated. An image
of workers' bodies, the floor tiled with aces, one-spot tessellations.
Another image of herds, or hordes, or heaps.

Self and severance, severance and care, care and unearthing,
unearthing and breath. A Venn diagram of good girls in orderly
queues and wild-haired cyclones; daughters of Sita staying put within
the chalk circle, emanations of Sati raining Himalaya to its knees. All
kinds of women pulped for symbolism, all kinds of skins. Overturn
it, consider the other side; it's for the poor beast's own good, the beast
can't know when it's done, or they did and went anyway, couldn't not.

In whose voice did you hear me ask, what's good? I can make out a
triangle or a pyramid. When the poem answers its own questions
about access, if getting it is like getting in, making it, it's not. A heap
of bodies, softer at the top. What do you remember about that time?
Standing with our own kind, forgetting what we'd spent our lives
learning about life, amnesia as the condition for progress. What
progress? Locked in columns of better: getting, being, rotting.
Kindness denuded. When the poem quotes, *there is no Hindu*

consciousness of kind, do the rats in their holes hear the caterwauling outside?

The painting was abstract to prevent you from seeing what's depicted, from thinking you might be in a position to see at all; a Venn diagram of disclaimers and rubber stamps, mass distancing, ratified oblivion. I'm going after like-mindedness, putting *us* on trial and paying tribute. The daughters' eyes flash fire. Assiduousness as the condition for inhumanity. They killed us to save us, suicide by kind, faces whitening in the scrape. No aphorism can declaw the problem, pin it down to be neutralized. An image of artworks and poems releasing spores, aerosols for ideas and impulses that germinate after the gallery or book is closed.

A great poet envisioned *ever-widening thought and action*, whilst you were forensicating nothing. But we were all, for a moment there, facing and feeling the same thing, grieving and writing about the same thing, and what came of it, that time, if something had to, did it? Do you remember? Say nothing's doing, capsize. Nothing's nothing to snub, as if migratory paths can be traced in the shape of a nose, no. What do our bodies have to do with history, and how does relation lend legitimacy, if we're all? Tenebrous bars, spitfiring wells. Soft heaps outside the city walls, forming a lethal periphery. The small rain down can rain all around the swallowing heart.

≻≻≻

what if we took an unravelling warp

    away from the kernel of bourgeois history
        (steeped in guilt, defensive walls can't dam its secretions)

    away from the essence of fascist-nationalist history
        (the rotten rope of destiny, manifesting against life)

    away from the stranglehold of stories told and retold, only to
    uphold *oneself*

ascending the sound of the spiral then

like, we really feel whales because we can hear them, because we can
imitate their song and think them mimics, we want to save them they
help us focus and sleep

we want to save them, they prosecute whiteness surfacing smile,
like

whale mouth berthing
upon ear sea
cleaver
brought to waxy
pasture endures *chemical*
cloud-mould of
audition
number crunch
inner incinerator screeves

or, spirals disrupted, a heap of eyelashes on the pavement,
crushed shells, is the family drama and these somatized
drawings and sound maps

is how I tried to describe it

when spelunking forgotten dreams

Stop just before the entrance, the sheet of running water or loamy smell. This is the last sunlit station; the rest is groove. The architecture of the cave helps people and animals sync up with space-time as well as with each other, like the internet shapes our built and social environments and is shaped by them. The finest paintings are far from the entrance, but no one controls the buzzer, you can call your way in. Call then; utter any silent sound or informational noise, the cave will respond. A little away, a little away; come close, come close. You can trust this voice, can you? You can hear your way to belief, the deeper you move in its stuff. Brush fingers, sticks, and bones against stalactites, compare the effects to xylophones or soundbars or whatever feels right to your sonic context. Stamp your muddy handprints on the walls, ceding your subjectivity to speleothem. Feel your way into millions of years of drip, flow, gush – never dry, never still – even if you cannot perceive the wetness and movement with your fingers, ears, nose – you can, you can. A shimmering carpet of crystals; an assemblage of golden eagles, porcelain skulls, bio-glitter, bhindi glue, lip melt, flute, fur. Every sound in space-time still resounds; every sound ever made leaves a scratch in the field; the field is the recording, every sound ever made reproducible. The air swathes warmer here, breath ripples further than you intended to go or thought possible. Maybe you'll ignite a torch to signal reciprocity; maybe you'll awake surrounded by bear scratches, horses, birdcages, shapeshifters, or by bears, artists, ceremonies, spirits. Will you dance, will you boggle, will you enter another kind of sleep? Here you are folded in; you cannot see or be seen, you are out of the state's earshot, beyond cannons and espionage. Here you can sleep for millions of years; borne by your secrets which will never be mined. You are the matter in which splendour is hidden; you are the sculptor who shrouds their work.

unpredictive body-2-body

crushed shell of the murex snail says this isn't a question of
perception, mostly, but questioning perception does help

we move with the problem of how snail says, how snail's saying is
projected upon, how snail's markings, mark-makings, are obvolved
by hermeneutics, so that paralytic effect becomes imperial property
becomes psychedelic breadcrumb

ask too loudly how to follow the astral trail and delete neural cookies
concurrently, like an improvised flight through Is-ness, then pundits
will step forward. so channel your questions through the microscopic
snakes that swim in your waters, and observe your waters' writing

we admit the inseparability of minds from their makers, having no
consensus on the nature of mind but conceding the culpability of
makers, or rather their investors, or rather the historical factors that
privilege some investments over others, or rather a soldering of a
form of investment (capital) with an ideology of value (racial) whose
power depends on violation and the extraction of other rinds and unds

what then? we can try listening to the sutures, admit that listening
is always mediated and it's no place to stop, whether through my
selective ear or your superseded dictionary or these crepitating buds
or those tritanium gales

the differences are more-than-affective and we can sense our way to
knowing something that's not an expansion of intelligence tracked
to informatic raids but precipitative, a transduction of the cloud of
unknowing into auroral strata

these shades of difference can be discerned, however wide the
umbrella, they can be named, however bumfly the fit, whatever
brings us closer to keeping them

then nudge keeping into the frame and fold frame into artwork, with
the borders deliquesced we can hover the problem anew. as listening
is always mediated, creativity is always framed; what artwork could
defy or obliterate perceptual limits, how to pose that question
without invoking scepticism, or simulation, or infinite regress

like, translation-as-metaphor all the way down, or we're language
models predicting what comes next, or everything is everything is
vibratile cilia

there might be an approach that doesn't retreat to preterition or
rigidity

try another rockpool and we find ourselves on a picket line, students
and staff chatting, chanting, pass the megaphone

we're here we free writing machines the next
word sparks a scene change juxtaposition
discovering new rooms in your body
new friends because they can't hear they don't
know we're getting bigger smoking them out

~~~

if name and form fuse, signs
proving things for things
stirring them into sensibility

as one can't lie to a telepath
how precisely we'd sound
how sound would consummate

    freeing data
                and

      triggering virtualities

a basket woven of one's own hair

Onomatopoeia is the containerization of the past in the present and future, the valorization of perfect rhyme at the expense of grain, the ratification of sameness in service of representation. The nameless dread attending onomatopoeia is the acousmatic monolithic that displaces reflective space. It's like a bathtub in a bathtub in a bathtub to infinity, without anyone to find the lyric-it and sing about it. Onomatopoeia may pose a grave threat to diasporic experimentalism for these reasons and more. Kukūnana [poet gargles on stage]!!! At a dinner party in the mirror universe, we're all played by fungi – beautiful, submarine, networked fungi – and a xenobiologist descends to catalogue us, channels our spore clouds, and eventually helps us converse. Our words and images tend to oscillate irregularly; what seems like blurriness from a distance is methodically bound up close.

L argues, the point at which sound reminds us of our corporeality is often the point at which sound is described as becoming noise.

you put your left vom in /// your left vom out /// vom in vom out /// you shake it all about

Difference as the radiant crown of body odour that can be perceived from a distance. Here's a sequence that spreads, an incrementally disclosed map of exclusions: bus ride, dance, tribunal. His nose crinkled condemnatory. The virulent splaying of hokey-cokey. White judge smiling at white manager smiling at the employer's white legal team; their neighbourly triangulation of racist deniability. Ooof.

D describes a correspondence between the racial policing of the experimental and the racial policing of the nation, asserting that the violent assembly of home and belonging is as much an aesthetic endeavour as it is a policy issue.

that's what it's all about /// that's what it's all about /// that's what it's all about

When most of our chats take place under water, not in the stars as I'd thought, we go buḍabuḍa-buḍabuḍa, dispensing bubbles to kiss. I say that I've let the ill winds in, they were already swirling inside me; you suggest an alternative, identifying flow as a stabilizing force. Sometimes observation is the healthiest form of participation in the sex dream, its outside balancing the psychic books. Poetry as the stuff that's cropped out of postcards; in the background, a congregation of wind turbines, dumped fridges forming a breakwater in front. Is the problem of categorization a problem with the production and utilization of categories or with the process of recognizing and responding to the problem itself? Because, in my favourite poetry, the object isn't more beautiful wrested from its source, and you don't get to cup it tenderly before crushing it. Because, if thinking is fucking, the leg of the stool is kicked out!

P writes, in a letter to an unaddressed addressee, we're far out to sea. The shell of the paper nautilus enables a state of buoyancy wherein the force of an object submerged in a fluid is equal to the weight of the fluid it has displaced. The liberty of internal renewal.

you put your right vom in /// your right vom out /// vom in vom out /// you shake it all about

You might feel foreign to yourself, as if hovering in front of your body and trying to lipread. Lyric-you and lyric-I look over there to see who's beaming in, leaving space to defend ourselves against them, if necessary; holding space to show that we can handle the unknown. That kind of poetry, like gigantic ears flapping against the window at night. Like living next door to the internet, once in a blue moon dropping by in your blanket of tongues, and licking reboot.

A and T ask, what is your current relationship to change? What does it mean to think of change as your god, and why does this question elicit resistance?

that's what it's all about /// that's what it's all about /// that's what it's all about

a poem's shadow (baskets in the mirror universe)

You know that feeling when words flee your body, the magnetic field of your tongue reversed by a touch, a demand, a jolt, and you lose the power to discern verbally let alone speak? The imperial silence produced by the *someone* inside fills you up, transmuting you into a vacuum for your own thought processes. Imagine a bathtub overbrimming with warm syrupy language that freezes and desiccates as soon as the *you* you've become climbs in. I'm trying to sing but my voice keeps leaving me, to teach me a lesson about place, property, and appropriate subject matter. I've done it again. Any simulation of mimesis is a trap. They want to bind you to remove you; it helps that you come pre-wrapped.

If I am read brownly, heard brownly, weighed brownly, what am I? Two agents from the Department of Temporal Investigations materialize to lament, *or whennnn*? So, skin colour is like onomatopoeia, insofar as limitless equivalence between sign, signifier, and signified are falsely insinuated. The encounter with onomatopoeia in the Sanskrit–English dictionary is enchanting. As if some words contain the echoes of their past, and in pronouncing a word correctly I can reproduce long-lost entities and activities. Individual words are acid-free boxes in the lexicographical archives, the carrier bag of stars.

But no, the atmosphere has changed since that dictionary was compiled in British India in the nineteenth century, the process of recording and conserving alters the words irreversibly, the grain of my voice renders an abortive soundscape. If the sound could exist now, then I could not, you neither. This isn't even getting to the conceptual paucity of identity and representation politics, and how these rely on the logic that you can only hear me if I sound like you, and how that logic destroys everything that might be beautiful in the world.

Somebody left the mangoes in the rain, and that's fine, and somebody else went snorkelling, and that's fine too, is a dead end for The Discourse; oh, make a way out of no way, let me be errant! Demystify inspiration, open wide and show your working. Think of all the conversations had about knowledge, difference, erotics; think about who spoke, who listened, who cleaned up. How many times have we talked about race? How many times have we received the advice to claim space like a mediocre white man? How many times have we reflected his image, inwardly and outwardly, without trying? The next line is an example of self-citation, filtered through a reference to a computer game designed by my friend, as if other-citation has the power to emancipate self from ego. Does it?

The game allows players to explore an ocean planet, taking samples of spores, stalks, and jellies to analyse at an abandoned research base. Before I learned how to play properly, I thought the objective was to eat the samples to fuel my diving suit, as an illustration of the colonial enterprise of scientific progress. But the dinner party also took place in our universe, with coordinates in space-time, and I need this filter to distance myself from the awkward turtles that stream out of my body when I recall the event. It's difficult to talk to people who are like you in such a way that the ways in which you are unlike are keenly felt, incomparably hurtful; here, I surface to admit that it can be easier to talk about race with white people, for anyone who wants to leave early, to quit without saving. But I will venture a *we* and stake everything (ego, credibility, lovability) on the eschaton of that pronoun – draw you in, tie you loosely in sandalwood smoke. Now you see us, now you don't.

It's kind of weird to be one of three, or two, or the only person of colour in a room and to meet the same white people repeatedly for them not to remember you – I'm the only *one* here! . . . it's just kind of weird, you know? Now mango, now snorkel; now *fuck you*, now *please*. If you've seen an ikat shawl up close, you'll know it takes craft to seem this opaque, it takes precision to achieve that subjective/objective blur. The geometric patterning of tongues and nodes, like a musical score. Schools of poetry are organized along racialized lines (and classed, and gendered), no doubt, but what happens to poetry when we historicize its instantiations and imagine it as unmappable space concurrently? What happens when we perceive the visual noise of brown and black people in a white room in conjunction with the syntactical and sonic noise of difficult poetry, understanding noise to be the message, and translation a means of relating that refuses assimilatory judgements of intelligibility. Scream in outer space, turn your body into a cetacean sound system.

I wished for no less as an observer at an employment tribunal. Sitting on the claimant's side, against my employer (her former employer), I observed the panel nil her disquisition of race and sex discrimination. The shadow o'erleaps itself; this sequence begins with an everyday experience of racism, as a teenager with her best friend on a bus in Glasgow, when a man told me I smelled like shit, over and over again. On our way to a party we were too young to attend; it doesn't matter that we'd spent hours getting ready, it doesn't matter that she's blue-eyed/blonde, it doesn't matter that he's drunk. White people can tell that a brown person smells like shit from far away, men can smell with their eyes, and it might be a superpower but it's not structural racism. Neither is the fact that not all children are born knowing how to do the hokey-kokey and may experience nausea when forced to take part.

On the other hand, and we're in a privileged realm here – the players are salaried and mortgaged – I swear I observed the white judge, the white counsel, and the white professor-manager smile at each other as the claimant spoke. I swear I observed their three smiles emanate like beacons, creating and suspending a triangle of light at the front of the room, spectacularly impervious to the brown woman giving evidence. Cameras weren't allowed, otherwise I'd show you. In the upset, everything becomes lucid; whatever you thought for however long was really the inversion. *Shocked! but not surprised.* 99 per cent of international data is transmitted by submarine cables; a network of cables laid on the ocean floor conveys messages between you and me, supports our friendship and our many projects. Xxxxxxxxxx's to infinity. How does the sound made by an object as it sinks change qualitatively throughout history; how is this bubbling sound, even *this* bubbling sound, not actually universal?

Alone in a big house at night, a woman comes downstairs to find the back door open. Are you scared? Don't be. The darkness that blows in symbolizes her admittance of the other, interior wickedness maturing into external forces such as poetry, communities, institutions. She becomes stronger in the realization that she is embedded, not mother superior, and bids goodnight to the trial. The observer effect reconfigures notions of the text that's open to co-production between writer and reader – everyone who looks casts different hues and tints on the scene, recomposes variously. As in physics, so in poetry; as in the poet's poem, so in the analyst's room. We're light years beyond the tabula rasa! Go ahead, feel free to look but not touch, eavesdrop but not attest. If you decide to write it down, don't think for a moment you're fixing things in place.

Scroll through your personal records and consider the degrees of curation. Do this again with nature poems. Is it possible to describe a stunning view in all its layers, according to the eco-poetics of totality?

The desire to include everything as a means of rescuing the would-be-righteous poet from their embarrassing poem is its own issue, as if the outside could offer the kind of salvation that's found when deemed irrelevant. The next bit is tricky to explicate, one sentence standing in for a conference paper. What's the problem?

Rather than get caught up in debates around linguistic innovation and the avant-garde, or mislead by personal preference and that already intimated siren, *taste*, let's rethink the problem's terms. We're not interested in winners, the ones who claim to arrive first as if arrival could be uncontested, as if origin stories are anything other than narratives of domination and expropriation and lengths upon lengths of archival silence. We listen harder, lest the sound of our fears and desires rings too loudly, shattering the traces of the ones who composed but didn't write, who wrote but couldn't publish, who published but weren't read, who were read but never *read* read. You get the argument; it hinges on categories and the slice of their fall. If beautiful poetry extended no further than appropriation, only the bullies could do it, plucking idiosyncrasies and resolutions as they saunter up the path to the ivory tower, pricking fingers to write elegies to lost blood.

Vom! Tell us where you found it unless you're punching up. The creative writing workshop as a diabolical factory producing faulty office chairs, the better to keep lines from working. In that sense, poetry isn't a big deal and it's everything. Maybe the dolly feels as many misgivings as we do, but does he know the psychic rift that opens when one's image of oneself is stacked appallingly with other's images, tremors threatening the dream of coherence? Probably, yes; although I bet his worthiest rivals look just like him. All these pronouns, and we're still unable to account for the relationship – when the lyric was first encountered, how to calculate the right moment for denunciation.

The truth is, it was already collapsing when I considered myself bold enough to belt, and I'd committed to other failures. Put your ear to the page, let the defectors crawl in whilst there's time remaining for discussion and the good humour to fly. Squelch the rest under the maul of their axiomatic velleity. Ultimately, there's an erotics of bewilderness and hyperconnectivity at stake – if you snip the wrong wire, it's smithereens. The grotesquery of aboutness, barring the door to entropy's music, rattling the structures that it's locked from within. S's hair smelled like citronella the last time we met IRL. Will you keep holding? Ask me again.

blood-roarer, via body's sympathic

this time you're metabolizing when you   *ha*
aṃ   begin no need of your many entrance
says this cave you don't need to visit to   *sa*
aḥ   know how do you know how do you prove you
sonospheric collapse spinal cord-wards   *ha*
aṃ   after particle hailstorm leaves pinprick
tunnels too many to count your centre   *sa*
aḥ   a tottering column of sea urchins
lightning antennae impinge from inside   *ha*
aṃ   out you are alone in your own body
illuminated by the fountain of   *sa*
aḥ   fire now listless now luring drollery
whoop bloody whoop bloody whoop bloody whoop   *ha*
aṃ   bloody bloody whoop bloody come come home

to your adventure your wonderland your   *sa*
aḥ   river snakes swim up amber bubble
bong ring your vital forces eddying   *ha*
aṃ   the stethoscopist hears your heartbeat not
your effluvious infrastructure not   *sa*
aḥ   your unsounded deluge meta-woofers
compensate for vasculotoxic care   *ha*
aṃ   his auscultation drawing a sonic
colour line around fugacity which   *sa*
aḥ   might mean brownian black voices noises
which might sign the zap of semiotic   *ha*
aṃ   gap the well-pronounced sound that produces
law otherwise latent in the nameless   *sa*
aḥ   dread attending onomatopoeia

˄˄˄

shapes oscillate to release the sacrificial logic
making a swarm of its perpetual motion clink

~ we gain in petals ~
~ revolt sunbeams bridge ~
~ feather the balance ~

wetly amass and taste without touching

~ ~ ~ wave with all our brains ~ ~ ~

hello

hello you

paths to enlightenment drawn in sand

CHILD [holding a stick]: How many worlds may be seen in the desert?

ARTHUR AVALON [holding forth]: Let us suppose that man's body is a vessel filled with oil which is the passions.

CHILD: If centres proliferate, what formula shows the blizzard's role in the poetics of relation?

ARTHUR AVALON: If you simply empty it and do nothing more, fresh oil will take its place issuing from the Source of Desire which you have left undestroyed.

CHILD: If the beach is burning, what of the adulterous woman's name?

ARTHUR AVALON: If, however, into the vessel there is dropped by slow degrees the Water of Knowledge (jñāna), it will descend to the bottom of the vessel and expel an equal quantity of oil.

CHILD: Who confers innocence to the potting-mix homunculus, to repossess its shit?

ARTHUR AVALON: In this way all the Oil of Passion is gradually expelled and no more can re-enter, for the water of jñāna will have wholly taken its place.

CHILD: What is so unabolishable about hierarchy, incarceration, destitution, death as cleaved from life?

ARTHUR AVALON: As the Latins said, if you attempt to expel nature with a pitchfork, it will come back again.

CHILD: What if there's no more nature, either because it's over or because everything is?

three for ahmad jamal trio

But Not for Me x Ahmad Jamal

a marble staircase ascends from seagull wings
inclement seas of teeth throw up a line
    so brief
    no time to think before
    being spooned
into the standards their moving messengers
    the line escalating into
– *just* – goodness – *just* – warmth – *just* – love – where you really
   wanna
    go where you must
it's a question of – mmmmm – a repertoire of mmmmms
getting in tune with the surroundings
separate tranquillity from illusion receive
that contribution that perfumed oil
of accidentals how is this melody held
    in strinkling
    this story told
    in gazillions
of tickles his discipline his constant discourse making something out of
   something
    discovering
what's already been created so precious – anchored
in the air in the unreal real experiment
    that's the real unreal peace
his extensions pouring the vessels of our bodies and rooms ooooo-eeeee
unburdened by the necessity of survival eye-catching pieces of
    patchwork continuum
but vamp this accompaniment with empathy

and assemblage of stored breath
there he goes
    there he goes
    there he goes
    o living music

But Not for Me x Assata Shakur

you describe your grandmother's dream
summ spa *summ* spa
women who struggle and tend spectrum
summ spa *summ* spa
who don't not know what freedoms mean
ma plush *ma* plush
hopes unmurdered murder impossibility
ma plush *ma* plush
you remember hope as better die aliving
hum chah *hum* chah
what's for you won't let you get used to it
hum chah *hum* chah
rainbow fingers spreading out the distance
lap luhh *lap* luhh
where wicked expropriation walks freely
lap luhh *lap* luhh

fictive judge seeks a prehistoric response
baa shpih *baa* shpih *baa* shpih *baa* shpih
based on the unnatural separation of soup
imm dot *imm* dot *imm* dot *imm* dot
understood as our genetic characteristics
dab chih *dab* chih *dab* chih *dab* chih
by the tentacled extraterrestrial engineers
ffilll off *ffilll* off *ffilll* off *ffilll* off

you name yourself opposer of opposition
duh shop *duh* shop *duh* shop *duh* shop
oh ksha *oh* ksha *oh* ksha *oh* ksha

       duty-bound in beauty to the line venceremos
yumm sop *yumm* sop *yumm* sop *yumm* sop
hohh ral *hohh* ral *hohh* ral *hohh* ral

bop fluhh *bop* fluhh *bop* fluhh *bop* fluhh
ulll jjoy *ulll* jjoy *ulll* jjoy *ulll* jjoy
llosh up *llosh* up *llosh* up *llosh* up
nub wonn *nub* wonn *nub* wonn *nub* wonn

But Not for Me x Hallāj

they're writing songs
of love but love's only
love's only only
united in the thing
itself not like you
and your body
but for life's curves
life's arabesque
accumulation of chains
he walks in desire
his only truth
a doxography onto himself
he walks in words
divinely inscribed
recites his truth
guts spilling on sand
in the melismatic form
of his name
letters braiding
dramatic events braiding
witnesses his name
having begun well
ends badly
the formula sealed
with a bloody kiss
where his ipseity
couldn't keep quiet
his loud love his union
in me although I can't
dismiss the interiority
of my dwelling

fingering the line
to open up a space
filled with boiling
soup well told anecdotes
rosewater memories
of birds long flung
lapidation alchemied
by art stones become
birds become ripples
where roses mark
the scatter of his ashes
in the Tigris tradition
divested by magic
well done in public
rationality counterpoised
with miraculous critique
with love to lead the way
let me be lost
unlike the truths
which I haven't known
beauty ecstasy stars
shadow's faces
in markets libraries
public gardens
the homes of booksellers
his profound mortification
teaches me
that I'm a bad friend
to my body
and no good thief
the only truth robs
selfhood from oneself
the truth patched

together by detractors
o cottonwool carder
of consciences
o surrenderer o discerning
o dazed o comb out
my shyness my stained
hearts o correspond
with me by each of my
names walk until you arrive
in the primordial dialogue
clairaudience making
your mouth froth
yellow grapes pistachios
wasp-attracting dates
the material continuity
of breath-pierced bodies
sweetly stung for social
purposes conversion
of harm to gracious
identification beyond race
believers finding themselves
in communities of love
supreme of love supreme
of love declaimed in ideas
in patterns laws
remembered recompose
the struggle for words
intussuscepted and set
twangling in air and
open forums

sita rama variations

Rama Katha

ever since leaving the key handed down to me
down to de-story these well-formed homes |

daśaratha nandana, father's gladness fathers' palates
irresistible blueprints ||

raghu kula bhūṣaṇa, ornamental family tree
the nation's non-conducting walls |

but heard again as hers-not-hers, the usherings of Turiya's retelling
softly coursing old-new names ||

sītā devī jīvana, she who fruits in furrowed mantles
lights incense in the underworld |

now Alice whispers and it's not for me, one hand earthing
the other unveilable ||

sītā devī mohana, she whose arrows unclog love and heartbreak |

the key changes, we're none of us out of the woods
all homeward bound to liberation ||

prema niketana, milky temple tender might |

in her cadence these gods fly planes and avenge across borders
hanumān mahadāśā, solidarity's best agents ||

pour desire into the fault-line network
one body's a hotpot but earth organs heat |

asura nikhanana, how the city of gods was de-rooted, razed still to
give, to give gladly
of brown study and palimpsests ||

rāmacandra balavat, I move in language like an antibody
lexicographer's apprentice, made small and warm by limit |

the origins of poetry, from crying out (śoka) to canny incremental
(śloka), skin-sleeked with moonlight in the dark forest of
renunciation, night-sky effuse ||

ayodhya līlā mahaye, she walks me across this fanciful derivation
the vehemence of gospel's aftersound not to be warred against
for heaven's within Us, harps nonstop |

how I imitate you playfully palms together
how you glissando the form of grace ||

triloka līlā mahaye, R&B ascetics in the clearing between stars
alone and never, the Supreme Being fudges and Alice won't let go of
these notes, My Names |

Turiya keeps time uncountable in the soundbooth
the fond bleeds of her footfall evergreen jasmine exudes – –

Si Ta Ra Ma

turn the corner into a signal jam, a holy man sitting cross-legged
on a bigger sadhu's tongue, rhotic adulations rolling between them
RAMRAM**ram**ram**ram**RAM**RAM** – a double counterpoint of nose-
to-tail singing and monkish parps –

> continue walking down the street
whilst looking back at the ritual – wah!

> a sea lamprey drops in and swallows the shot –

> rearing up to catch your eye, the open
palm of his voice guides you to the music that's playing athwart –

> Moki's banners unspool Carnatic solfeggio,
syllables inscribed on loose-leaf teeth – **ah-knee-sah-rayyy** – Don's
doing it different, get magic-carpet comfy in the grooves his rule
breaks make –

    pah-ree-gah-maaa tambura charges the air, tabla gives flight –

> **si-ee-eee-taaah si-ta ra-ma si-ta raa-maa**
children break in and sillystring the band, scuffing the chalk marking
stage or home –

> we're unseated and clambering,
feelers spill off the sides – **mmm mmm mmm hmmmm** to fuel the
elephantasy, this composite body soundtrack – acrobatic limb
ladders, sense organ plaits – no nerve –

> **money-sari-sunny-prop seagull-null-me-runny-bah** –

> time's currents correspond to the contours of
defences, wild gardens, forests, we're flying phantasmagorical against
gloss! mountains, a healing herb range –

> no nerve –

> **13 14 15 16** virtuosic where you
are with what you've got – if feeling and enumerating seem
incommensurable – then infant joy! – **saintly silky multikulti** –
gong bath in homophones, pomp in oblong glory – **tuk tuk goo goo
goose** – no nerve! – diyas light the intervals between us, our colours,

o happy day – no wait,

    warp! –

        tunnel shrinks in trumpet's soliloquy **shhh** nested throat
keening **shhh** aureal squawks quarks walks – wounds cool in steelpan
shower – players carousel, reigning and reining in, bowing the better
to hear –

                              piano chords skim the big top,
cream pluck spins off, leaving us lacunal, uncapped –

                                   drumsticks clatter –

                  form yawns –

～～～

    housecats on the windowsill
       quacking at parakeets
         in the silver fir parrotfish
     knit intestinal rainbows

                    R quotes the strandentwining cable of all
                    flesh in a chat about navel-gazing as
                    contemplation of the celestial placenta into
                    which we're all plugged

        around the same time we walked around time,
                              time's pass

we walked to Ladywell and back giving way to dogs, enjoying the
patter-bounce-echo of paws on the spiral bridge

shirking on rented space-time

the space where the class war occurs as such is, in its pure form,
    imaginary as we hold
on to this one you won't find another aquilegia like this
        imaginary in the mathematical sense
words inadequate to pink mouse dreamwork
the shell suit god lent you bursts open to highlighter blue,
     rosehips on the doorstep, Haribo wrappers
        wherever you stand to smoke – discarded crops
our jobs pay for this downstairs neighbour
     to play Nightswimming again our jobs pay
for this acoustic-guitar guy whom I didn't invite
     to my party who didn't invite me to his *towers of set-theoretical*
universes
        that can be controlled through relative
    consistencies, like

bedtime, work hours, nonbeing apportionment
     like oil and comb hair before jumping through flames
confined to a small region of space we
react to our confinement by moving around
     kittens rescind my order, perform air hockey with bangles
each surface a sonic minefield, or else
   I watch my neighbour watching the neighbours clap
     I cannot speak about the situation without speaking about
myself, most-liked sources for this long fix
     rewound breakdown from *small, self-centred units*
     to polymorphous membership at idiorhythmic hearths
each does their thing undampened, plays Endgame with friends
        Ah yesterday!   we still can pap, elegiacally

redeem these loyalty points
               these gilded bindings

      side effects of institutionalization are effects of institutionalization
            Thanks for letting us know
            about the asbestos, we really
            appreciate it! rent asunder clouds
dipsomania reveals so much about clouds
morbidly, the natural world   hellebore coursing through
      vasculature
sentiment's a tourniquet, edducing *save me* a dewdrop
in the socially ultimate ocean, future peoples serving flow
of love unimpeded by species or skillset
      primula essence, flaxen hair hammocks, spiral age playlist
            tending each other's mysteries, we'd leave our mouths open
not because of policy, Simon says
      our landlord is not a mega-wealthy property magnate so no
we can't stop paying rent

maintaining these notions, these networks, these recreationally
      stratified
      nights in
since the rending of embodied copresence
      contact's out the window   miss atomic meet cute
      window became mirror   miss bygone olfatronics
      mirror lost its mandate   miss the 4D bus to Mattapoisett
            when we future conditional enjoy a little more and less
      destruction
of personal space, an embolism in the communal organism
unless you're using it to pray says The Architect of the Matrix
our landlord, not everyone needs to puncture their necks
      to prove the poem's truth, but
            the ghoul did squinch at a mooncup pop

the lard really did turn blue!

I'll leave you, it's time to clean always, to apologize, to reply   the
   fruits

of my labour endowing how many fruit bowls   off stage

muddy rivers (filthy tributaries)

ginger cymbals but flies
skip and send trilling
confounding dome

it's beartrap city, one of its many hearts
mirrored blades dice mirrored butterflies
one bug says, writing is piping through

sewage, an atonal motion that foments
plots to escape – and static. can fire
touch the fire in my pocket of time

stay unquenched in the vacuumed sky
another bug, a nice snail, asks nicely
I salt him back. I square the piny collar

that oyster-souls may pass intact. bugs
lie, digest, slime trails gash in this city
and better animals get hurt. if we're

going to leave, we have to leave now
we have to clean first. you say, look, I
get it, but now you need to stop. charge

render spirit vacuous
enervate matter, longed
for cryospheric break

throw out a line of voice – herring shoal
in a basement! hear soft glints curdle soft
clumps pall, they must wick to watch

performance is the shoal swimming
back in time, returning with bulletproof
teeth or leaving you screaming off stage

faces lit up in the blazing trash. but
all memory comes to your side
for the theophany little soldier boy fades

into dunkleosteus, wraiths smash wings
in the dust in the windowless room
the diva charms, her harmonic sprangs

bang wallop into walls, condensation
blueing, remember the scene, blue
scales plasma'd to sky-sweating walls

> *razor clam sensorium*
> *oil-painting-thick sky grip*
> *licked open to blues*

see how easy to disappear completely
how to forget the moonraker lasers
of love that made me, the competition

that's love. if you ask where we should
meet. one more time, if you ask bivalves
to hold unsustaining notes, moments

the line emits break the chain of choice
the world is cold, thorns; I am thorns,
flames, blue; other people electric blue

hoops, fumes, air. loving you betrays
their system of being, the gesture rudely
jubilant, our death in mode-switching

metal crescendos our incendiary
requiem. then say what's for you severs
you, lull noticing lull and notice must

> *red algal buster sorry*
> *to be dead and still standing*
> *fingers pullulate-leave*

anent precenting the line

this city, where the millionaire capital passes the murder capital
in the street, nods without smiling at its own reflection, clutches
its purse, the matrix of chicken tikka masala's self-renunciation,
conveying the fancy for imperial rule, sows' ears made from tar

what those great men gave up on behalf of their children
to find fortune in graves, to propagate unnatural names

leveraging their inheritance: don't just subsist by learning,
strew the clearing with the bright lights of benevolence

rivers like biomimetic circuitry of extraction,
            shipping routes spread out from Glasgow
                                    like the ribs of a fan

enlightened bystanders are on hand taking questions on looting
as red-cloaked nation strides past, the inevitability
        of his gold-tipped cane, proselytized

attending to the story that is mystified yet
totalizing at the expense of counter-nations

the nation (to which, of course, the people
who have been converted do not belong)

children must give thanks for being sacrificed,
the profits of their destitution sight unseen

the story that might be better known yet
under-studied, the city teaches us to look

up

– following a line down Albert Drive – where cultural contact springs up like forest – marking the spots that require unearthing – ornament is grafted on the hardy and resolute – pinky, pista, and jalebi sticky the tramway tracks with Glasgow's other colours – whilst fair-weather temperaments construct themselves as foreign for mutual reward – at every strata in the terms of the rich – crossing Shields Road towards Victorian mansions built strong enough to hold ceilidhs in the attic, so say letters sent back home – admiring this nominal relationship to the flower and whispering to find out what complicities it tends – if the *noble passion* is free to claim or denounce – insofar as nobility is limitless when sequestered from power, there is a jaw parallel to the ground – defensive posture compromised as the nasal cavity is exposed, a midge might dart in, or a more sinister fleck – crypto-zoological beasts do more than line their nests with tartan – men who were moved moved to move other men, another outline that distracts from the matter – through the ghosts of cotton mills in Pollokshaws, martyrdom's composers – all echoes might be seeded with fractal paisleys – unravelling in a manner diametrically opposed to Draupadi's sari, that is, unravelling – like the beloved juxtapositions that adumbrate violence and disavow reparations in the eyes of liberals – but roots move differently, sound out reckoning's blur, fathomless causes and effects beyond geometry's key to history – *I am not here, then, as the accused; I am here as the accuser of capitalism dripping with blood from head to foot* – cheery and dangerous, or cheery because dangerous, a Scottish link in the golden chain of world socialism – a mile and a half from where I grew up, feels closer today –

M concludes, LET US SUFFICE
TO SAY THAT IT IS THE SURVIVOR
OF THIS TALE THAT HANGS OUT
HER STORY TO DRY ON THE
WASHING LINE OF REMEMORY

in surviving she gives out the line
that a chorus might be drawn as these
subjects are to more heat than light

in giving she tunes the repetition
unbleached dresses still dripping trade
winds knotted with workers' songs

in telling she coruscates the web
lapses flash to do undid interactions
Syrcas restores the bending touch

H says, in a discussion about slavery and the forms of relation produced by its perpetrators, I'm wondering if the whole society didn't escape, if abuse became the order of the day. We must stop what we're doing and down our critical tools. Her remark is our event is the world's gravitational field. Without thinking about it, thus letting go of it, we might try to feel what entanglement means, with and without touching, with and without the capacity and liability of being touched. Invoke the vertical plane to confine the inquiry to tobacco lords and their sons, or forsaken clanspeople and evictees, or planters, or soldiers, or inheritors of the ancient universities, accountants, doctors, clerics. Notice how these images reflect and contort according to what holds up the mirror and who stands before it, how the question of a nation's truth can limit the reach of its answers. Extinguish the wall with the supreme understanding that walls are not found in nature, which is this inquiry's unconfinability; a spiralling formulation that allows us to sustain the project thanks to regular stoppages and explosions.

does not ev en con tain your name
does not ev en con tain
the mat ter of your name in sound
in sound as in rest less

ness as in res pon ding with warmth
if your name could give out
like song in flight to the tem ple
of truth vib rat ions seats

flocks re turn black ened sound ing
the het er o phon ic
range of your names ex is tence can't
con tain your be com ing

        this song a text you'd keep writ ing
        on this cir cle a cy
        mat ic de mand to fol low each
        line to the ends of time

        to their buds you'd go be yond work
        be yond sub ju ga tion's
        false friend ship hills col lapse in to
        red cen tre burn ing dock

        buds bridge bridg es sing back your steps
        you don't go pre vi ous
        you go tubes with in tubes pull through
        and min gle free dom clues

we can say back we can say for
wards our say ing bod ies
green skies milk strike ma ny good arms
un cross en tranced stretch time

our nat ur al names spo ken with
love dis perse side real ly
call back to earth worms groove so cial
life through out un i verse

        ir re du cib le div ine line
        for got ten race ri ots
        re al co op er a tion cho
        rus of can't take it do

                ech o les son in ten der ness

～～～

say the Divine Ear must be dissolved

    divinity isn't the pondering hand that compounds the
inequitable, measuring out breath in disposable cups

        isn't the missionary's boot, but the microbial
        symphony on the sole of his boot

    all those lifeforms without eyes and mouths, who comb
      and branch inconceivable

inside the long string instrument we vibe

eroto-magnetic shockular
merrying that mode
of bumping
to music whilst
walking off riffing on
poem-machines
anti-grave
licence universal
all you have to do is dream

we'll track each other
over Rajasthani
quilts two
aliens exploring
ice sheets in concert mind
speech travelling
circumlunar
creating spectacular
lay finespun under solidus

most harmonic lattice
lined filter beds
read as music
meander through
these bars or moveable
nuts granite tune
temperament
whilst playing with
them magic fingers free

time is all about walking
in the intervals
covering
each other skirts
seams burst paroxysmic
space is finding
definition
inside lines poeticule
showboats spectrum in earnest

a submarine sandboxing match

if the figure was glitchy before, now it's positively defrag-screening,
bricks breaking into meteoric swirl; although we love each other,
everyone looks white

is it strange that all colours look and sound different underwater, the
water column as kaleidoscopic tube, but whiteness remains constant in
the dark, white noise scintillating above the surface, or is it obvious

our words keep bubbling away from us, precision is nut-cracking
down here where brains scoup spongily, but we need to air this so we
can think it together: race is not a perceptual phenomenon, yet race
may be perceived by the sensory organs (all of them, yes!)

race is not a perceptual phenomenon, yet racism is frequently
perceived by the sensory organs – try again – racism is frequently
perceived by the sensory organs of the ones who perceive racism

not all sensory organs have this capability, implying that some people
have extrasensory perception – no way! – extrasensory perception of
the mundane order

what do people with tinnitus and yogis and poets and racialized
people have in common

like acute embarrassment, punchlines have the power to stop time

allowing us to stay here for a while, to try some things out; say,
musical diffraction, so that oceanic feeling becomes oceanic listening
(we make the briefest stop for fuel at noise-cancelling oneness; don't
open the doors, the platform's too short)

the Deep Listening Band starts playing, in a welcome if not subtle
overture

can we deepen the ethical valence of listening as close listening or
paying attention by conceiving of listening as openness, dissociated
and absolutely attached, committed and unhurt by repeated
interruptions, overwhelmed and able to rest whilst rocking

this would entail listening across scales and sonic environments,
to voice messages and bloops, classrooms and firmaments, briny
lifeforms and arid heart-furrows, atoms and Ātman, and so on
and so forth

remember the oceanic isn't a continuous state, although it gestures
towards a particulate-indivisible continuum

we'd need to integrate the Listening-Is-Always-Mediated subroutine
in the programme

the figure, sick of being forced into shapes conceivable by humans,
like all those sentient noncorporeal beings in outer space, leaves us
swattering in our senses and conveys the argument telepathically

no, it's not strange, we agree

mmms for organic music society

we could put our ears to the flotsam and jetsam, cracked doorways to ocean the listening this listening could be

> *like echo untethered, now gaining, now space-cruising*

>> *sci-fi whales like mythological swans like world historical elephants sing, hah-mmm-sah-mmm*

> *help us! somebody help us out!*

let's go away from formal miseducation, golden faces pressed between pages, that schooling in the development of underdevelopment, that naturalizing of disunity; away from the servant of severance and all such passive constructions, amass the never never nevers till all are free! but, about, who? they'll check the balances in heaven, right? how many skies?

> *what if we felt a groove, ah-ah-ahhh, it's the simplest song, all the children know it!*

let's sing to ourselves, send selves back where shadow falls evenly, undo the lies that silence binds, furrow and furl every surface

> *ah-aye-I swallow radiolarians, pinpricks of light to pattern the throat, make a song of splinters without predetermined source*

> all you hear at the heart of hah-mmm-sah, infinity's chiasmus

and we'll walk through the clouds of us, wet in the mist of us, crystallizing the dance this decision could be

smudges of breath, cracked faces in doorways, the unravelling
bundle that sings at the hearth

ah-ah-ahhh to chorus the warp
to warp the contours, woah-oh-oh-oh-oh

unfolding maps of ascension's tracks

᭦᭦᭦

page drips
   to inquire
with associative
   sewage

snoticles twizzle
   bungee back

and this possibility shouldn't be ignored

      the suspended discord
      strung with ultrasonic bells
      and comb-jelly lights!

      a crab-wise island
      sand produces vertigo
      a claw-pocked sky

liner notes

it's probably raining in heaven

is the last line of a poem I can't hang on

to a torn flag maniacal against the skull of my mouth

an augmented reality

broch launches cracking the viewfinder

    allowing the soul to U-NO-what

a real swan

solitary in the lochan

    real sheep grazing on selkie landings

    never blameless

to naturalize their presence makes elegy

history or instead historicize the spat hangnails

of sign-makers

undermine

the mines of mythopoesis o how low

    poems make us how they body dream

organs from engines trumpet make-do tambourines

    looking outside for sources in recycling bins

answering machines

it's me she's leaving messages

not inclined to be

    there

no need to reply immortally casual

tearducts give me thin air and booklungs

give me a muse who can do both

outsource responsibility choose erotics

of the social this birdcast songweb spelling over us

this time we

walked in Eriskay I'd sat and watched for seals

with a stranger's ghost on the Scilly Isles

in the girly continuum of blue doors

my jai mā pendant rendered

choice unworkable

in wedging the ribs of the vault

I resigned to words' wills afeared of ill will

not the bright contagion of mingle

but muckering to pickle or milk

this sounds beautiful but

what does it mean say gap desirer say line lamenter

it means the muse's children are living

it means she's still in debt

hearing Rama's story in Alice's voice

Sita transposed to H.D.'s Eurydice not taking out on

the way down rather carrying her

paints and pastels within

her apricot swish turn on stage

home doesn't come naturally

stage lives that begin in the years ensuing your birth

conjugate the home or homes that wrote you

the ship's captain ploughs air

    inspirates freely

amidst this seafoam combustion of missing women

and absent friends

    there is a kind of strength

in not being driven by gratitude

in attempting not to survive

let's not valorize it but hear what listening leaves us

soul unchained sore rub rust

shipwreck ears

slaked with buttercups

nothing really bothers her channelled sideways

    or straight down

but *she just wants to love herself* doesn't fly

because when I learned that my treasure was found

buried in the absence of my or your misfortune

the earthy breath of my election when I hurt my

self or you swabbed the shore no nothinged

    every single footprint in the sand to follow

    hymns no more

in this fallaciously originary

pre/historically fertile place pitted by fairies

caved in by rack-rent

who you come from hemmed in

by oceanic potential and defunct phone boxes

    all the notes you could hit with monkey bridges

between Indo-European muster

R showed me the word svarabhakti in a book

of Hebridean waulking songs

the devoted or parasitic vowel in Gaelic one such

bridge a platform to linger in syncopation

    a little late

    a little dislocated embraceable

you or I take the high or low road

try to stay dry under the jellyfish bell

echo-shower-sting all the way back

I wanted to write a poem to rival medusa

to author the shapelessness of love

    given

reauthoring the bog of my nightsky

lit up by the being and the being of cottonwool

underlaid by all life and all death gridding deviant

sky erupting with lichen

    without godding

hearing the Ramayana again it's a story of this

way that way over and under mothering

many stories, all of them spindrift

many voices, all of them loved

we read Stephen's poetry to the birds at the farthest shore

as we'd read Callie's poetry to the birds at the farthest shore

there's probably a rainbow somewhere on earth

    not here

ᨑ

going past the personal

    imagine words' promise   makes it to the moon
    surfs earth's wave to   get so far out of reach
    how brightly it flees   draining light as it cools
    far from where there's   no walking outside ruin

and keeping going

    we traipse silkily and pratfall
    between merbears uranian
    humpbacks

    suspiration
    between ear bubbles
    ocean whisked in skullcap

darkness casts horizons

more for alice (vibrations too demanding)

What happened to Alice?

Huh?

What happened to Alice? Where did she go?

Turiya inscribes,

> January, February, March 1969. As ordered by the most divine Lord Sri Rama, these months consisted of regulative engagement in tapasya with tests of endurance, receptivity, and resistance that included days and nights of wakefulness necessary for examining tolerance to heat and cold, fire and water, electrical and magnetic energies.

> October, November 1969. On certain days, the Lord sent me travelling between obscurity and Infinity.

> January, February, March 1970. Lord Sri Rama stated that these months will consist of past lives' review accompanied by a series of tests. Afterwards, there would be intrafractory rays, audible oceanic and abyssal waves interspersed with astral magnetic frequencies – terrestrial and subterranean – brought to bear upon the mind. This was very interesting.

> April 1971. On this fine day, the most holy Lord Rama said, 'With the flame of tapasya, the incense of the soul burns, aromatically sacrificing itself. There is a luminosity of the soul that becomes increasingly enhanced moment by moment. While the incense burns, its perfume ascends sacrosanctly

toward Me . . . As it burns itself out, it is consumed by Me; and the sacrifice is enjoyed by Me.'

If *he* wanted to be the opposite, then what did *she*—?

Do you want?

Do you want Me?

Picture a mother too bright to look at directly; the
image is inevitably overexposed, her children
remember so little after the outline, the way her
brightness strayed outside the lines of her body.
They remember that she listened to butterflies, that
her rashes spread to shrink their debts. Picture a
teacher too *beyond* to communicate plainly, whose
visitations can't be reconciled with hospital visits,
whose aloneness is the lesson, her differential
populous, conducting anchor. A good girl with a
strong work ethic; a woman in love, on the edge,
more children than friends; an otherworldly woman,
clock-breaker, no-thing-namer, grieving in a language
she doesn't speak, symphonizing realms of silence
and rapture, overleaping and receding in the wakes of
inscription, her divine revelations, her altru-vista.

Picture a workbench close to the boundary but
inside the city's walls, a body hunched over in a style
that marks labour, or rue; that image is replaced by
a silhouette of two figures, framed by the window,
out of sync in their embrace; then a drop-leaf table,
sahasrara-like it could extend to seat the whole world
at a dinner party, but there are only four chairs. Like
the rainbow that circumscribes the happy family,
the matriculated ones – a mirror image of the lovely
sky boat that portends other logics. Look up, what
seems to be the zenith from below is a blowhole,

and us in the belly of hell, and us delivered by the
whale's breech, and our ears, like seashells, *still
multitudinously murmuring of the ocean* as we flee
through spiracle, as we fountain, glitter, celestify.

What of the righthand path?

The righthand path?

The righthand path –

Alice plays the piano as if light weighs less, crinkles in the skin
of the sky mean the possibility of repair and thus return

Eyes open, open window to the Magnificent Hands, wind's
fingers lashing, fire whip, light years fizzing between us,
our encounters, sunrise too quick, sea rises too quick, hits
sky, the sound of many smiles alighting, melting, gaping
holes in sky, Get up! Get up! there's no home like your face,
no sun like that, no need to come, will Be, Why would
anybody want anything else if this is a possibility?

What of the lefthand path?

The lefthand path?

The lefthand path –

Alice plays the piano as if darkness travels slowly, the echo bears
witness to singularity, corroborates its transitions

Bones huddled, footbound, rock strung, luminous message
turning to shadow as written in sky, mantles lowing in the
field, whereby hand may be heard long after hands left, the
pianist a glove puppet for love, the harpist an atomizer, the
organist unbeamable, out of range of the direct home line,
etiolated by their unclean hearts, mine interfering with
others' messages, telephone ringing so relentless that tides
learn tides, Then let me believe that!

Is this Me? Is this not-Me?

Who's asking?

two hands playing at once
and dispersing – a haunted
mask, a healing mask – all
you can't discern sustains

me. how often performing
spells an end to panic, or
begins a new sentence; go
through the looking glass

2 become 1 with the Self,
i.e., background noise. Alice:
mother-teacher-bandleader
is the figure 4 in her trio,

Turiya not a pose most can
make, or hold for long –
she's different. deferential, I
ride with my head out the

window. she's holding,
audience scales her up; in
the quaver between vistas,
costume change, set change,

sea! she's still holding, and
in all temporalities of love
and justice, wind brushes your
face, so grow up. swami

appears in the cracks of
broken sentences, showing
how to be in that non-
redemptive state of soul,

No Arc Zone. you're different
teach me. the teacher you
seek as the limit of what you
can learn. claggy and aloof,

my selves squabble over Me;
I'm dropped eggs and she's
walking on ahead. at the end
of the corridor, a clearing –

the lessons you're given as
the horizons of what you
deserve. pomegranate grove,
will-o-the-wispish bridges

    bits of song
  juicy specks
              there she goes,
                    back into the infinite –

~~~

alone-together-alone on the percipient superhighway
dipping into each atom-interim-star
immersions obliterate distinction, for the time being

everything we long to hear at once and gone
ears worming away from language that wrongfoots, compels

snip!

snap!

snorum!

waves snow-cresting against rocks
one body sways on the path
others firework, neither shared nor hampered
                    in the funereal knot
ever made and always shared in the nauseous pop

acknowledgements

Fantasia is an attempt to chart flights of fancy, to document experiments born from personal and collective study, and to score correspondences, real and make-believe. The manuscript paper finds its music in the people with whom I write.

Sarah Shin, who published my first book, *States of the Body Produced by Love*, has made more possible for my poetry than I can express. Talking with Sarah, going with her into the mists, discovering portals upon portals, and generating finite rules for cosmically expanding games, has been one of the transformative journeys of my life. My gratitude for Sarah's peripatetic genius. Thanks to Ignota, especially Jay Drinkall and Susanna Davies-Crook.

Patrick Farmer invited me to write about the cochlea, to think of the ear as an organ of multiplicity and an environment through which we can move, quoting Fred Moten talking about sound as an 'intense engagement with everything, with all the noise you've ever heard'. I was finishing *States* and struggling to make my way out. Moten's work offered a clue, a rackety bridge that I imagined extending between Tantric Poetics and Black Study, erected by footsteps in air, each step promising a descent to the depths. There are numerous teachers on the rackety bridge, but only one guide, Alice Coltrane, or Turiya (in her Sanskrit appellation), whose music transmits the fundamentals. Patrick's invitation sent me the spiralling images necessary to make the crossing, and his own love-led work not only makes me sensible to the aurality of my body but struck and full of gladness at being amongst other beings in the world.

It was thunderbolts for days at Arika's Episode 10, A Means Without End, and I relearned how little it's possible to know, and how

88

unlimited the possibilities of thought, when we devote ourselves to entanglement and the realisation of counterintuitive realities. Thanks to Barry Esson, Bryony McIntyre, and the magnificent team, and to everyone who revelled and groaned in the fug.

Thanks to Sarah Hayden, I had the opportunity to be poet-in-residence at John Hansard Gallery as part of the group exhibition *Many voices, all of them loved*. Curated by Sarah, the exhibition featured contemporary art that questions who speaks, what constitutes voice, and how technologies enable, manipulate, and obstruct hearing. The title is from Peter Manson's poem 'Time Comes for You'. I'm grateful to Peter for all he teaches us about deep time and silly noises. Thanks also to Dianna Djokey and the Interruptions/Disruptions writing group.

Several of these poems began during the lockdowns in 2020 and 2021, during which time I fell in love with *Star Trek*, initially as a means of travelling across space and time whilst stuck at home, later for critical lessons in utopia's failings. This was also a period of online reading groups, whose texts, discussions, and moments of connection and rupture, so keenly felt, suffuse this book. Thanks to all of them, short-lived, occasional, and ongoing.

Thanks to Anne Duffau for inviting Ignota to take part in Wysing Polyphonic's Under Ether, and to Sarah for extending the invitation to MJ Harding and me. I am still reeling from our collaboration *Treble Heaven* – our tentative processes and audaciously high notes – and am indebted to Mikey for what he teaches me about wholeheartedness in attention, performance, and presence.

I'm grateful to curators and arts organisations for commissions to run workshops and to develop and perform my work: Critical Poetics and Nottingham Contemporary; Sonic Art Research Unit, Oxford

Brookes; Centre for Contemporary Arts, Glasgow; Kunstinstituut Melly; Mythopoesis for Techno Living Systems, Academy of Fine Arts, Vienna; Sonic Poetics and Café Oto; Haus der Kulturen der Welt; Rupert: Alternative Education Programme; From the Lips to the Moon; Autograph Gallery and Bagri Foundation; SAVVY Contemporary; Aural Diversities.

Early versions of these poems appeared in the following publications, with thanks to the editors: *Almost Island*; *Azimuth, the Ecology of an Ear*; *MAP Magazine*; *Flatness*; *The Hythe*; *Erotoplasty*; *Carrier Bag Fiction*; *Spam Zine*; *JUF*; *Soot Breath/Corpus Infinitum*; *How to Sleep Faster*; *Wasafiri Magazine*; *The Penguin Book of Modern Indian Poets*; *Ludd Gang*; *The Senses and Society*; *Now's the Day, Now's the Hour: Poems for John Maclean*.

It has been a pleasure to work with Poetry School, Arvon Foundation, and Ledbury Critics, and I'm grateful to these organisations for their support. Thanks to the School of English and Drama at Queen Mary University of London for enabling me to spend time in the Isles of Scilly and Uist, where this book found its movements. I am in awe of colleagues and students who refuse the terms set by the institution and make other kinds of study, passion, and collective power manifest daily, especially Zara Dinnen. Thanks to Guy Robertson and Mahler-LeWitt Studios for the vivifying gift of space, wonder, and attentiveness, to everyone who sustains the studios, and to my co-residents and collaborators in Spoleto and beyond. My sincere thanks to Granta for making *Fantasia* exist in the world.

Here's an incomplete list of influences and allusions in *Fantasia*, in order of appearance and not accounting for variations and revenants: Fred Moten, Alice Coltrane, Pauline Oliveros, Swami Pratyagatmananda, Justice P. B. Mukharji, Franya J. Berkman, Arthur Avalon/Sir John Woodroffe, *A Sanskrit–English Dictionary*,

Theresa Hak Kyung Cha, Sarah Hayden, *Star Trek*, Bhanu Kapil, B. R. Ambedkar, Urvashi Butalia, Reena Saini Kallat, Rabindranath Tagore, Walter Rodney, Stefan Helmreich, *Phantom Power* podcast, *Moby Dick*, *Cave of Forgotten Dreams*, Matt Parker, Will Alexander, Darko Suvin, Édouard Glissant, Jackie Wang, Ursula K. Le Guin, Fernando Zalamea, *In Other Waters* computer game, Laura Chernaik, Octavia Butler, Renee Gladman, Nathaniel Mackey, Ahmad Jamal Trio, Assata Shakur, Hallāj, Simona Sawhney, Don Cherry, Moki Cherry, Ticklepenny Prawnmobile and Worf, James Joyce, Samuel Delany, Marge Piercy, Radiohead, *Peter Grimes*, *In Our Time* radio series, T. M. Devine, *Capital Vol. 1*, John Maclean, Denise Ferreira da Silva, Arjuna Neuman, Peter Manson, Robin D. G. Kelley, Shola von Reinhold, H.D. and Bryher, Nirvana, Stephen Watts, Callie Gardner, W. G. Sebald, Shankari C. Adams, D. S. Marriott.

Z is Rehana Zaman, L is Laurel Uziell, D is Dhanveer Singh Brar, P is Patrick Farmer, A and T are adrienne maree brown and Toshi Reagon, S is Sarah Shin, R is Robert Kiely, M is Maud Sulter, H is Hortense Spillers.

Finally, my love and thanks to the poets and friends who make community more than a fantasy, with whom I've been fortunate to talk endlessly, share work-in-progress, collaborate, and caper, especially Edmund Hardy, Laurel Uziell, Tom Betteridge, Emilia Weber, Nat Raha, James Goodwin, Eley Williams, Holly Pester, Gloria Dawson, Will Harris, Mary Jean Chan, Jay Bernard, So Mayer, Karenjit Sandhu, Ryan Ormonde, Sejal Chad, Georgie McVicar, Erin Lui, Špela Drnovšek Zorko, Benjamin Thompson, Leah Jun Oh, Derawan Rahmantavy, Robert Hampson, Andrea Brady, Isabel Waidner, Generative Constraints, everyone involved in Subtexts, and in loving, moony memory of Callie Gardner. It's been a dream to work with Rachael Allen, puzzling together over this book and much more besides, and I'm thankful for her perspicacity, strength, and exuberance. In real time, *Fantasia* was mostly written with Robert Kiely, fellow space traveller and guide in exactitude, my ground and sky.